ADOPTIVE FAMILIES

Families Today

Adoptive Families

Disability and Families

Foster Families

Homelessness and Families

Immigrant Families

Incarceration and Families

LGBT Families

Military Families

Multigenerational Families

Multiracial Families

Single-Parent Families

Teen Parents

Families Today

ADOPTIVE FAMILIES

H.W. Poole

MASON CREST

Mason Crest
450 Parkway Drive, Suite D
Broomall, PA 19008
www.masoncrest.com

© 2017 by Mason Crest, an imprint of National Highlights, Inc. All rights reserved.
No part of this publication may be reproduced or transmitted in any form or by any
means, electronic or mechanical, including photocopying, recording, taping, or
any information storage and retrieval system, without permission from the publisher.

MTM Publishing, Inc.
435 West 23rd Street, #8C
New York, NY 10011
www.mtmpublishing.com

President: Valerie Tomaselli
Vice President, Book Development: Hilary Poole
Designer: Annemarie Redmond
Copyeditor: Peter Jaskowiak
Editorial Assistant: Andrea St. Aubin

Series ISBN: 978-1-4222-3612-3
Hardback ISBN: 978-1-4222-3613-0
E-Book ISBN: 978-1-4222-8257-1

Library of Congress Cataloging-in-Publication Data
Names: Poole, Hilary W., author.
Title: Adoptive families / by H.W. Poole.
Description: Broomall, PA : Mason Crest [2017] | Series: Families Today | Includes index.
Identifiers: LCCN 2016004539| ISBN 9781422236130 (hardback) | ISBN 9781422236123
(series) | ISBN 9781422282571 (e-book)
Subjects: LCSH: Adoption—Juvenile literature. | Families—Juvenile literature.
Classification: LCC HV875 .P64 2017 | DDC 362.734—dc23
LC record available at http://lccn.loc.gov/2016004539

Printed and bound in the United States of America.

First printing
9 8 7 6 5 4 3 2 1

TABLE OF CONTENTS

R0446948038

Key Icons to Look for:

Words to Understand: These words with their easy-to-understand definitions will increase the reader's understanding of the text, while building vocabulary skills.

Sidebars: This boxed material within the main text allows readers to build knowledge, gain insights, explore possibilities, and broaden their perspectives by weaving together additional information to provide realistic and holistic perspectives.

Research Projects: Readers are pointed toward areas of further inquiry connected to each chapter. Suggestions are provided for projects that encourage deeper research and analysis.

Text-Dependent Questions: These questions send the reader back to the text for more careful attention to the evidence presented there.

Series Glossary of Key Terms: This back-of-the-book glossary contains terminology used throughout the series. Words found here increase the reader's ability to read and comprehend higher-level books and articles in this field.

In the 21st century, families are more diverse than ever before.

SERIES INTRODUCTION

Our vision of "the traditional family" is not nearly as time-honored as one might think. The standard of a mom, a dad, and a couple of kids in a nice house with a white-picket fence is a relic of the 1950s—the heart of the baby boom era. The tumult of the Great Depression followed by a global war caused many Americans to long for safety and predictability—whether such stability was real or not. A newborn mass media was more than happy to serve up this image, in the form of TV shows like *Leave It To Beaver* and *The Adventures of Ozzie and Harriet*. Interestingly, even back in the "glory days" of the traditional family, things were never as simple as they seemed. For example, a number of the classic "traditional" family shows— such as *The Andy Griffith Show, My Three Sons,* and a bit later, *The Courtship of Eddie's Father*—were actually focused on single-parent families.

Sure enough, by the 1960s our image of the "perfect family" was already beginning to fray at the seams. The women's movement, the gay rights move- ment, and—perhaps more than any single factor—the advent of "no fault" divorce meant that the illusion of the Cleaver family would become harder and harder to maintain. By the early 21st century, only about 7 percent of all family households were traditional—defined as a married couple with children where *only* the father works outside the home.

As the number of these traditional families has declined, "nontraditional" arrangements have increased. There are more single parents, more gay and lesbian parents, and more grandparents raising grandchildren than ever before. Multiracial families—created either through interracial relationships or adoption—are also increasing. Meanwhile, the transition to an all-volunteer military force has meant that there are more kids growing up in military families than there were in the past. Each of these topics is treated in a separate volume in this set.

While some commentators bemoan the decline of the traditional family, oth- ers argue that, overall, the recognition of new family arrangements has brought more good than bad. After all, if very few people live like the Cleavers anyway, isn't it better to be honest about that fact? Surely, holding up the traditional family as an ideal to which all should aspire only serves to stigmatize kids whose lives differ from that standard. After all, no children can be held responsible for whatever family they find themselves in; all they can do is grow up as best they can. These books take the position that every family—no matter what it looks like—has the potential to be a successful family.

That being said, challenges and difficulties arise in every family, and nontraditional ones are no exception. For example, single parents tend to be less well off financially than married parents are, and this has long-term impacts on their children. Meanwhile, teenagers who become parents tend to let their educations suffer, which damages their income potential and career possibilities, as well as risking the future educational attainment of their babies. There are some 400,000 children in the foster care system at any given time. We know that the uncertainty of foster care creates real challenges when it comes to both education and emotional health.

Furthermore, some types of "nontraditional" families are ones we wish did not have to exist at all. For example, an estimated 1.6 million children experience homelessness at some point in their lives. At least 40 percent of homeless kids are lesbian, gay, bisexual, or transgender teens who were turned out of their homes because of their orientation. Meanwhile, the United States incarcerates more people than any other nation in the world—about 2.7 million kids (1 in 28) have an incarcerated parent. It would be absurd to pretend that such situations are not extremely stressful and, often, detrimental to kids who have to survive them.

The goal of this set, then, is twofold. First, we've tried to describe the history and shape of various nontraditional families in such a way that kids who aren't familiar with them will be able to not only understand, but empathize. We also present demographic information that may be useful for students who are dipping their toes into introductory sociology concepts.

Second, we have tried to speak specifically to the young people who are living in these nontraditional families. The series strives to address these kids as

Meeting challenges and overcoming them together can make families stronger.

sympathetically and supportively as possible. The volumes look at some of the typical problems that kids in these situations face, and where appropriate, they offer advice and tips for how these kids might get along better in whatever situation confronts them.

Obviously, no single book—whether on disability, the military, divorce, or some other topic—can hope to answer every question or address every problem. To that end, a "Further Reading" section at the back of each book attempts to offer some places to look next. We have also listed appropriate crisis hotlines, for anyone with a need more immediate than can be addressed by a library.

Whether your students have a project to complete or a problem to solve, we hope they will be able to find clear, empathic information about nontraditional families in these pages.

—H. W. Poole

Steve Jobs, the cofounder and former chief of Apple Computer, is just one of many highly successful people who were adopted as young kids.

Chapter One

WHAT IS ADOPTION?

The founder of Apple Computer, Steve Jobs. The actors Marilyn Monroe and Jamie Foxx. The musicians Louis Armstrong, John Lennon, and Faith Hill. Former U.S. presidents Bill Clinton and Gerald Ford, plus First Ladies Nancy Reagan and Eleanor Roosevelt. Former South African president Nelson Mandela.

What could all these people possibly have in common? They were all adopted. Some, like Steve Jobs and Faith Hill, were adopted into new families when they were babies. Others, such as Bill Clinton and Jaime Foxx, were

Words to Understand

biological parents: the woman and man who create a child; they may or not raise it.

custody: legal guardianship of a child.

foster: to raise a child that is not legally or biologically yours.

informally: not official or legal.

kinship: family relations.

neglect: not caring for something correctly.

adopted by members of their own families (Clinton by his stepfather, Foxx by his grandparents). But all their stories show that adopted kids have many different kinds of lives and can grow up to be anything they want.

TYPES OF ADOPTION

Adoption is when a person (usually a child but not always) leaves his or her birth family to join another family. Beyond that very basic definition, there are many different types of adoptions that occur. The different types are determined by three factors: who is doing the adopting, who is handling the adoption process, and who is being adopted.

- **Public.** A public adoption is one that is handled by a part of the government called the child welfare system. Sometimes **biological parents** willingly give up all legal rights to their child; other times the child is taken away from the parents because of abuse or **neglect**. In public adoptions, the entire process is guided and paid for by the government.

- **Private.** A private adoption, on the other hand, is handled by an independent agency. Adoption agencies connect people who want to adopt with children who need parents. In these situations, it's usually the would-be parents who pay for the adoption.

- **Family.** Sometimes, when parents are not able to look after their kids, other family members will step in to help. This situation is also called *kinship* care. In some situations, the family member will formally adopt a young relative. But other times, the situation is a bit more loose. A child might simply live with an aunt, uncle, or grandparent, even though the biological parents still have legal **custody**.

- **Stepparents.** Another type of adoption can occur after a parent marries a new partner. That new partner is called a *stepparent*, and sometimes he or she becomes a legal parent of the kids. Whether or not this happens usually depends on the relationship that the kids have with their biological parent.

- **International versus domestic.** Adoptions that happen within one country are called *domestic adoptions*. For example, an American child is adopted by Americans, a Canadian child is adopted by Canadians, and so on. But sometimes adoptions happen across borders—an American family might adopt a Chinese child, for instance, or a Canadian family might adopt a child from Ethiopia. These are called *international adoptions*. About 8,600 foreign children were adopted by American families in 2012. That total is way down from the peak year of 2004, in which there were almost 23,000 international adoptions. The drop is mostly due to other countries—especially Russia and China—placing limits on how many adoptions are allowed.

- **Younger versus older kids.** A lot of parents dream of the day when they bring a baby home from the hospital. For that reason, it's pretty

The actor and musician Jamie Foxx was adopted by his grandparents when he was about seven months old.

When a parent is in the military, kids might stay with other family members (kinship care) until their parent comes home.

common for parents to adopt babies, as opposed to older kids. A lot of private adoption agencies specialize in placing newborns with eager adoptive parents. However, there are about 400,000 American kids in the **foster** system—meaning, they are living in group homes or with temporary families. A lot of them are hoping to be adopted, too.

- **Transracial adoptions.** When parents of one race or ethnicity adopt a child of a different race or ethnicity, this is referred to as a *transracial adoption*. At one time, transracial adoptions were very controversial , because many people believed that children had to "match" their parents in terms of race. Some experts still worry about what life will be like for kids who are raised by parents who don't share their background. Can they, for instance, identify with problems of racism and discrimination that may occur. But transracial adoptions have been gradually increasing since the 1950s. The 2010 census found that about 40 percent of all adoptions in the United States were transracial. (For more on transracial adoptions and matching, see chapter three.)

CARING FOR KIDS

Sometimes it's impossible for parents to take care of their kids. They may have financial problems, issues with drugs and alcohol, or some other challenge. Some teenage girls who get pregnant realize they are too young to give their children the best lives possible. Other times, parents might be serving in the military, keeping them away from their children for long periods of time. The same is true of those sentenced to time in prison.

When these things happen, the obvious solution for many families is kinship care. It has been estimated that about 2.4 million Americans are caring for the children of relatives. The majority of these caretakers are grandparents. It can be overwhelming for grandparents to have young kids again after so many years. But experts say that kinship care is better emotionally for kids than care by

Understanding the Numbers

You might be wondering, how many adoptions are there every year? Or, how many adopted people are there in the United States? Unfortunately, these questions are a bit tricky to answer.

For generations, the adoption process was kept very secret. The U.S. census didn't even ask about adoptions at all until the year 2000. Because of the secrecy, and also because some adoptions are done **informally** within families, there is no exact count of how many there are.

But we do have some data that are based on public adoptions, as well as information gathered from private adoption agencies that are willing to share their success rates. From these sources, it has been estimated that about 125,000 adoptions occur every year. Experts believe this figure has been declining since the 1970s, when there were roughly 175,000 adoptions every year.

The 2010 census counted approximately 1.5 million adopted children in the United States. However, it's important to be aware that census results depend on *how* people decide to answer the surveys. Some people don't identify their children as adopted on census forms, even if they are. Other people call their children "adopted" even though their kids are only informally, but not legally, adopted.

strangers. Unfortunately, kinship care is not possible in every situation. That's why other forms of adoption are so important.

People adopt for a lot of reasons. Sometimes it's because they want to have kids but are physically unable to do so. According to the Centers for Disease Control and Prevention (CDC), about one in eight American couples have trouble getting pregnant. Also, people sometimes make the decision to be parents later in life. They may have focused on their careers in their 20s and 30s, and it's only later that they are ready to raise children. Same-sex couples also sometimes decide to adopt (see page 34 for more on this issue).

Meanwhile, there are some 400,000 kids in U.S. foster care at any given time. Some parents decide to adopt simply because they want to help out kids in need.

THE ADOPTION PROCESS

Just as there are many types of adoptions, there are also many ways adoptions take place. In America, adoptions are handled by the states, and in Canada they are handled by provinces. That means every state or province sets its own rules for how adoptions can happen. If the adoption takes place within the same family—if grandparents adopt a grandchild, for example—the process may be fairly quick and easy. International adoptions, on the other hand, can be very complex and take months or years to finalize.

Adoptions within families are often fairly straightforward.

One prominent adoption agency estimated that the adoption process takes an average of 15 months from home study to placement.

So there's no single way adoptions happen. But these are some general features of most (if not all) adoptions:

- **Home study.** Usually, parents who want to adopt must undergo what's called a "home study," in which a social worker or other official investigates how the parents live. This usually involves one or several interviews with the would-be parents. There will be questions about family background, health, employment, and parenting experience. The reasons would-be parents want to adopt will also be discussed. The social worker also visits the place where the child will live, to make sure that it is safe. Most U.S. states also require that would-be parents take classes as part of the process. Home studies are required for all international adoptions, and for most domestic adoptions as well. Foster families also have to do home studies.

- **Finding a child.** Once the home study is complete, would-be parents go through the process of finding a child to adopt. (Of course, this step does not apply in situations where the parents already know the child, as in kinship adoption.) The placement process can be handled by private agencies. Parents can also use public services such as AdoptUSKids, a nationwide program that connects kids in foster care with would-be adoptive parents. How long the placement process takes depends a lot on what kind of child the family hopes to adopt. Parents will often have to wait longer for a newborn baby, for example, than for an older child.

- **Official placement.** When would-be parents have found a child who seems to be a good fit, they will visit the child several times, so everyone can get to know each other. If the decision is made to go forward, the child will go to live with the parents, and the parents will file legal paperwork that says they are ready to adopt. The adoption will be finalized by a judge.

Text-Dependent Questions

1. What are some of the different ways adoptions happen?
2. Roughly how many adopted kids were found by the 2010 census? Is that number completely reliable? Why or why not?
3. What is a home study?

Research Project

Choose one of the people mentioned on the first page of this chapter, and find out more about his or her life. Write a biography, and discuss whether or not adoption influenced the course of this person's life. Give reasons for your answer.

This 1663 painting by Jan de Bray shows an orphanage in Haarlem, the Netherlands.

Chapter Two

THE HISTORY OF ADOPTION

It's safe to assume that as long as there have been parents and children, there have been adoptions in one form or another. But adoption didn't always look the way it does today.

For instance, adoptions were fairly common in ancient Rome, but they were totally different from modern ones. Adults who didn't have any children would

Words to Understand

assimilation: blending in to a new culture and forgetting the old.

eugenics: the philosophy that the human race can be improved by controlling who gives birth.

genocide: deliberately killing a large group of people, especially members of a particular ethnic group.

heir: someone who is given another person's wealth and social position after the other person dies.

indentured servitude: a practice where someone agrees to work for someone else for a certain period of time.

subsidize: to pay part or all of the cost of something, such as living expenses.

adopt an adult male, usually a slave, to become their **heir**. Adoption in Roman times had nothing to do with finding a baby to love, and everything to do with passing on the family name. Later, in medieval Europe, orphaned or abandoned children could be enslaved by whoever took them in. These "adoptions" had nothing to do with building families. They were economic and labor-related decisions.

It wasn't until the 18th century that children were considered to be deserving of special protection. In 1741, the Foundling Hospital was established in London, England, for "the education and maintenance of . . . deserted young children." The Foundling Hospital is briefly mentioned in the classic novel *Oliver Twist* (1830) by Charles Dickens. In the book, the orphaned title character doesn't get to live in the Foundling Hospital. Like many real-life orphans in this period, Oliver ends up in a workhouse. Workhouses were brutal places where the poor of all ages had to work long hours for little or no pay, just to have a place to sleep.

EARLY ADOPTIONS

Adoption in the modern sense has its roots in the 19th century United States. Massachusetts passed the Adoption of Children Act in 1851. This law, which was the first of its kind in the nation, made judges responsible for placing orphaned children in "fit and proper" homes. In the 1860s, the Massachusetts State Board of Charities began **subsidizing** orphans so that they could live with families rather being placed in institutions. In New York City in the late 1800s, a charity called the Society of St. Vincent de Paul created the Catholic Home Bureau, which arranged adoptions for Catholic families. (The organization, now called Catholic Guardian Services, still performs this function today.)

This practice came to be known as "placing out," meaning that the child was taken out of the institutional setting and placed with a family. Children could be placed out temporarily or permanently. In that sense, the "placing out" system was the beginning modern foster care and adoption. However, placing out was

Kids working in a potato field in Minnesota. In the past, adoption was as much about gaining a new worker as it was about getting a new family member.

As American as Adoption?

Some scholars have wondered why the United States was the first country to implement the modern concept of adoption. For example, the Adoption History Project at the University of Oregon points out that while Massachusetts passed an adoption law in 1851, Great Britain wouldn't have similar legislation for another 75 years.

One theory is that Americans were more open to adoption because freedom of choice is a particularly American value. Unlike so many European cultures, where one's lot in life was determined by birth, Americans have long believed that people can choose their own fate. Maybe that's why America pioneered the modern adoption, in which a family is created by choice.

not *exactly* like how things are done now. Importantly, many of the kids who were placed out were expected to work. For those children, placing out was as much a system of **indentured servitude** as it was adoption.

Between 1854 and 1929, a quarter of a million children from the East Coast were sent to work out West as part of the Orphan Train movement. Farmers who needed extra help would go to the local train station or court house, select a child, and simply take him or her home. There is no official record as to what happened to most of these kids. We do know that some became happy members of their new farm families, while others ran away. And not all of the children on the Orphan Trains were orphans at all. Many stayed with their farm families for only a short time before returning to their biological parents back East.

EARLY 20TH CENTURY ADOPTION

In 1898, Columbia University offered the very first class in a new field called "social work." The first social workers tended to be upper-class white women who were concerned about the many problems affecting the poor. These women opened facilities for recent immigrants called "settlement houses." They also fought for limits on child labor, and they argued on behalf of women's right to vote. Some social workers opened the first private adoption agencies, such as The Cradle in Evanston, Illinois. The modern adoption process owes a great debt to these early efforts.

But the early agencies and the people who ran them were, in many ways, products of their time. That is, they held certain beliefs that most people find distasteful or even offensive today. For example, there was a widespread belief in the practice of **eugenics** in this era. The word *eugenics* comes from the Greek for "well born." Eugenics is the idea that the human population can (and should) be improved by encouraging "superior" people to have more children, while discouraging "inferior" people from doing so. Terms like "superior" and "inferior"

Girls learning to sew at a settlement house in Providence, Rhode Island, in 1912.

Indian Boarding Schools

As European-American settlers pushed the borders of their country farther and farther west, they found themselves uncomfortably close to the Native Americans already living on the land. This "Indian problem," as it was known, was usually solved violently. A native population of about 12 million in the 1500s was reduced to fewer than 250,000 by 1900. It was, in the words of the historian David E. Stannard, the "worst human holocaust the world had ever witnessed."

By the late 18th century, many people were arguing for a more humane solution. They believed the answer could be found in forced **assimilation**. At first, Native American children were sent to white-run schools during the day and allowed to return home at night. However, it was believed that Indian parents were still teaching their children "too much" of the native languages and customs. Instead, young native children were taken away entirely and placed with white families, or they were sent to so-called Indian boarding schools. About 100,000 Native American children were forced to attend these schools, and untold more were put up for adoption with white families. It has been estimated that between 25 and 35 percent of Indian children were taken from their families to be adopted by whites.

This practice was brought to an end by the 1978 Indian Child Welfare Act. However, some Native American child welfare advocates say that the practice continues today. For example, Native Americans make up 13 percent of the population of South Dakota, and yet they are more than 60 percent of the children who are removed from their homes.

were defined by factors such as race, ethnicity, and wealth. People were very concerned about the possible "bad blood" of the orphan population, and they felt that "inferior" children should never be passed on to "normal" families.

Eugenics went out of fashion during World War II. Adolf Hitler was a great admirer of eugenics, and the eugenics philosophy became associated with racism and with the **genocide** of the Nazi regime. Meanwhile, international adoptions gradually became more popular. Babies were adopted from Germany after that war, and then from Korea after the Korean War. This was the beginning of modern trends toward international and transracial adoption that are such key parts of adoption in the 21st century.

Text-Dependent Questions

1. How were adoptions in ancient Rome and the Middle Ages different from modern adoptions?
2. What was the Orphan Train movement?
3. What were Indian boarding schools?

Research Project

Research pictures of the Orphan Trains online and create a collage with captions explaining the details of each image you find. If you don't have access to the Internet, write three to four journal entries, imagining yourself on an Orphan Train being sent to a new place and family.

In the 21st century, we no longer assume that family members ought to all look alike. But this has not always been the case.

Chapter Three

TRENDS IN ADOPTION

Beginning around the 1920s, the adoption of babies and very young children became more common. These children were considered new members of the family, rather than workers or charity cases. Historians have speculated that loss of life during World War I (1914–1918), as well as an influenza epidemic, may have encouraged more families to adopt young children.

Whatever the cause, these adoptions were usually guided by a philosophy called "matching." The term refers to the idea that an adopted child should "match" his or her new parents in terms of race, ethnicity,

Words to Understand

consensus: agreement among a particular group of people.

diversity: variety; here, in terms of race, ethnicity, and other social characteristics.

indistinguishable: when it's impossible to spot the difference between one thing and another.

stigma: a wrong belief that something is bad and shameful.

intelligence, religion, and even physical characteristics. In the past, matching was extremely popular, but these days, fewer and fewer people care about it. Understanding this evolution is the key to understanding how adoption works today.

TO MATCH OR NOT TO MATCH?

The idea behind matching was that adopted children would "disappear" into their new families. Ideally, an adopted child would be **indistinguishable** from a biological one.

A few important things followed from the matching philosophy. The first was that the adopting couple had to be a married man and woman—it takes a woman and a man to make a baby, so you had to have one of each in order to

The philosophy of matching holds that adopted kids should be from the same ethnic group as their adoptive parents.

Rejected

In the past, adoption agencies worked extremely hard to make adoptions invisible. For instance, a woman over 40 could not adopt a baby, but she *could* be considered for an older child. That's because the adoption would be more "believable," since she might have had the baby when she was younger.

Here is a sample rejection letter from files held at Columbia University; it would have been sent to a woman over the age of 40 who wanted to adopt a baby:

> *We have given your recent letter telling us of your wish to adopt a baby very thoughtful consideration. . . . Since most of our children are the very tiny infants, we feel that for the present we must limit our applications to those families where the mother is under forty years of age. If we are able to increase the number of toddlers or older children coming to us, we will be happy to consider an application like yours. . . . Should we get a substantial number of older children, we will be glad to get in touch with you and discuss your interest further.*

Source: Adoption History Project. http://pages.uoregon.edu/adoption/archive/SLFAIWWOFYA.htm.

adopt one, too. Unmarried people and same sex couples were out of the question. In part this is because it was considered wrong for them to become parents, and in part it was because the child could never "match" them.

In addition, the woman had to be young enough to believably have given birth (see sidebar). The adopting couple and the child also had to be of the same racial and ethnic background. So, ideally, an Irish American family with green eyes would only adopt an Irish American child with green eyes. (One key exception to matching involved Native American children, but there were political reasons for this; for more on this issue, see chapter two.)

From roughly the 1920s to the 1970s, matching was the overwhelmingly accepted approach to adoption. The philosophy did attract criticism, however. In 1960 the social worker Justine Wise Polier argued that matching created a "wall of prejudice" that kept children from finding loving (if different-looking) homes.

OPEN OR CLOSED?

Matching required a high level of secrecy when it came to the child's biological parents. After all, if a child's adoption is meant to be invisible, that required the birth mother to "disappear." Biological parents had no say over who adopted their children. Adoption agencies held all the power in deciding which child was placed with which family. Meanwhile, adoptive families knew little or nothing about where their children came from. Birth records were completely sealed and largely impossible for families to access.

This type of adoption is now called "closed," meaning that the different parties are not in touch with each other. Closed adoptions were invented in the early 20th century as a way of making middle-class families more willing to adopt poor children. Remember eugenics from chapter two? If children came from "inferior" families (which could simply mean poor), then parents might not want to adopt them. But if the children's pasts were erased, families found it easier to view their adopted children as blank slates. In essence, everyone (the family, the birth mother, and the child) could more or less forget that the adoption ever occurred.

OPENING UP

Things began to change in the 1970s, for a few reasons. First, the **stigma** against single mothers began to fade. Previously, the idea of having a child without being married was a source of shame. But as that changed, fewer women gave up their babies for adoption. Suddenly, adoptable babies were in high demand. This meant that mothers who *were* willing to let their babies be adopted had more power than before. Birth mothers began to insist that they had some say over what families raised their children.

Meanwhile, adults who had been adopted began to wonder about their birth parents. Who were they? Why did the adoption happen? Adult adoptees began to try to change adoption laws so that they could get answers to their questions.

By the 1990s, these trends had given rise to "open" adoption. In the open system, birth parents and adoptive parents know each other and stay in contact. How much contact there is depends on the specific families. Adoptive parents might just share photos of the children, or they might call or write the birth

There are more people who want to adopt babies than there are babies to adopt. This means that pregnant women have more power to choose the future families of their children.

parents occasionally. On the other hand, some birth parents visit their children regularly and are even considered to be part of the family.

There is no "right" way for an open adoption to go. But no matter how much contact occurs, the point is that an open adoption is never treated as a secret. Many supporters of open adoptions argue that this eliminates the sense of shame that has hung over adoptions in the past. Today, about 80 percent of adoptions are considered "open" to some degree.

CELEBRATING DIFFERENCE

In 1994 the U.S. Congress passed the Multiethnic Placement Act. One of the law's goals was to end racial and ethnic discrimination in adoptions. These days, people are much more willing to embrace **diversity**. We know that a happy family does not need to be a "matching" family. This has opened the door to types of adoptions that were unimaginable just a few decades ago.

Transracial Adoption. According to census data from 2010, the United States is home to more than 400,000 transracially adopted kids. A transracial adoption creates what's known as a multiracial family. There are well over 5 million such families in the United States today. Although their numbers are large and growing, multiracial families still face unique challenges. In particular, kids who grow up in multiracial families sometimes feel torn as to which race or ethnicity they "truly" belong to. Some people worry about kids losing their original backgrounds when they are adopted into a family of a different race. (For more on these topics, please see *Multiracial Families* in this set.)

LGBT Adoption. Just as people once argued against transracial adoptions, they also used to argue against adoptions by members of the lesbian, gay, bisexual, and transgender (LGBT) community. Indeed, the very idea of LGBT adoption was unthinkable to many people for a long time, and it remains controversial to some. Technically, LGBT adoption is only illegal in Mississippi. However, some states have laws that forbid adoption by unmarried couples, which has been a barrier to LGBT adoption in the past. Now that that same-sex marriage is legal throughout the United States, the ban on unmarried couples no longer presents such a big obstacle to LGBT adoption.

There has been controversy about whether LGBT parents can be good parents. Both sides have pointed to studies that support their views. In hopes of settling this once and for all, a 2015 project at Columbia Law School began to collect every study that has been done of LGBT parenting. The project found 77 studies that found kids of LGBT parents turn out just the same as kids of straight parents. The Columbia team found only four studies that claimed kids of LGBT parents turned out worse. The American Sociological Association agrees. It stated that "scholarly **consensus** is clear: children of same-sex parents fare just as well as children of opposite-sex parents." (For much more on these issues, please see the volume *LGBT Families* in this set.)

Text-Dependent Questions

1. What does the term "matching adoptions" mean?
2. Why did people support matching adoptions before, and why do fewer people support it now?
3. Name some types of people who couldn't adopt in the past, but are now able to.

Research Project

Use U.S. census data to find out more about trends in adoption. Use the data to create charts, graphs, or maps that show information about adopted kids in each U.S. region or state. You could also use the census data to make charts about international adoptions. Or you could make a world map that shows which countries adopted kids come from. (For help, see the report *Adopted Children and Stepchildren: 2010*, available online at https://www.census.gov/prod/2014pubs/p20-572.pdf.)

It's totally normal to feel bad about adoption sometimes. Talking about it can help.

Chapter Four

CHALLENGES

As discussed in earlier chapters: adoption used to be viewed as a big secret. Birth parents sometimes felt ashamed that they had not kept their children. Adoptive parents sometimes felt ashamed that they could not create children in the traditional way (through pregnancy). And adopted kids sometimes felt shame because, first, they had been "given away" by their original parents, and second, they might not be the "real" children of their new parents. Of course, not everybody felt this way all the time, but those feelings were pretty common.

Fortunately, times have changed, and we know that adoption is nothing to be ashamed of. Families can be made by choice. When parents choose a child through adoption, they love that child every bit as much as children who are created through pregnancy. That doesn't mean it is always easy to be adopted. Even though there is no real reason to feel bad about adoption, people sometimes

Words to Understand

agency: the ability to act in ways that change a person's circumstances.

external: things that involve a person's relationship with the outside world.

triad: something with three parts; an "adoption triad" includes the birth parents, the adoptive parents, and the adopted child.

feel bad about it anyway. This chapter will talk about some of the common feelings and issues that come up surrounding adoption.

CORE ISSUES

In 1982 the social workers Deborah N. Silverstein and Sharon Kaplan wrote an article that explained their view of seven "lifelong issues" related to adoption. The point of the article was to try and help people better understand the emotional issues that arise for people whose lives are touched by adoption.

One interesting thing about the seven issues is that they apply to everyone in what's called the *adoption* **triad**. In other words, whether someone is a birth parent, an adopting parent, or an adopted child, these core issues are still important.

Some adopted kids wonder what their lives would have been like if they had stayed with their birth families.

Growing a New Type of Tree

Some teachers like to assign a "family tree" project to their classes, where each student draws a tree that has branches representing various family members. But drawing a family tree is difficult—and sometimes impossible—for kids who were adopted. Other teachers give assignments like, "make a collage of baby pictures." Again, this assignment can be impossible, embarrassing, and even painful for adopted kids.

For that reason, experts suggest adjusting assignments so they are more inclusive. For example, the "collage of baby pictures" assignment could be changed to "a collage of family pictures." Likewise, there are different types of "family tree" designs that can be used, such as a wheel that has the child at the center and all his or her caregivers as spokes.

(The examples below will focus on adopted kids only.) According to Silverstein and Kaplan, those issues are:

1. **Loss.** Adopted kids often feel the loss of the biological family they either used to know or never knew at all. Sometimes an event as seemingly minor as Mother's Day can be upsetting for adopted kids. Family-oriented events like Thanksgiving and Christmas may remind kids of the parents they no longer have. Meanwhile, school projects like "make a family tree" can make adopted kids feel "different" or "less than" (see sidebar on this page).

2. **Rejection.** It is common for adopted children to feel rejected because they weren't kept by their biological parents. This situation is never the kids' fault—adoptions happen for all kinds of reasons. But kids might feel rejected anyway. Adoptees might also fear being rejected by their adopted parents sometime in the future.

3. **Guilt and shame.** All three members of the adoption triad may feel guilt related to the adoption. For example, adopted kids might secretly believe

that they somehow "deserved" to be given away. They might wonder, "What did I do wrong? Did I cry too much? Was I bad?"

4. **Grief.** We tend to think of grief as the sadness people feel when someone dies. But we can also feel grief for things that never existed at all. For example, abused kids might grieve the happy childhood they didn't get. It's normal for adopted kids to mourn for their biological families, even if they've never met them.

5. **Identity.** Unlike the first four issues, identity is not an emotion but a state of being—it's about how we see ourselves, and how we interact with the rest of the world. Adopted kids sometimes worry that they are outsiders in their own homes. Yes, they are a part of their new families, but they may also wonder if they would "fit in" better somewhere else.

6. **Intimacy.** Having a sense of intimacy means that you feel close to those most important to you, that they make you feel safe and accepted. Adoption can make intimacy more difficult. For example, kids who were adopted might have trouble trusting others, because they fear they'll be rejected again.

7. **Mastery/control.** Silverstein and Kaplan's final issue relates to what people sometimes call a *sense of agency*. If you have a sense of agency, it means that you feel confident that you can make decisions that will affect your life. If you lack a sense of agency, it means that you feel helpless, like nothing you do makes any difference. Adopted kids sometimes feel that there is no point in trying to control their own lives.

Silverstein and Kaplan wrote about the seven core issues to try and help people better understand the effects of adoption. It can be very helpful to know that feelings like guilt or rejection are totally normal. It may also make an adopted person feel better to understand that other people in the same situation go through similar things.

Every person is different, and every family is different, too. Not every person or family experiences all the core issues. Or, people may feel some of these

It can be helpful to talk to people who have been through situations similar to your own.

things for a short time, but then not feel that way anymore. But understanding these issues can be a really important step in making peace with adoption.

COMING TO TERMS

Silverstein and Kaplan's list can help parents and kids understand some of their own feelings about adoption. But adopted kids also have to deal with **external** issues. For instance, if you were adopted transracially, your parents might look a lot different from you, and sometimes people might make comments or ask where your "real parents" are. You might feel weird when your parent picks you up at school, and everyone else sees how different you look. It's a good idea to talk to your parents about these feelings. Together, you can come up with strategies about how to deal with awkward situations when they happen. Maybe you can even plan a clever reply to people who ask silly questions about your "real" parents.

Case Study: Liza, Derek, and Elena . . . and Rosa

When Liza and Derek got married, they knew that adoption would be part of their lives together. (Liza had health issues that meant she could not get pregnant.) After they'd been married for three years, they decided to adopt Elena, a little girl from Guatemala.

At first, the adoption seemed to be going forward without a hitch. Liza spent hours staring at the pictures of the baby who would be her daughter. She and Derek longed for the day when Elena would finally be able to sleep in the crib they had ready for her.

But it turned out that Elena's birth mother had never signed the document giving up her rights to the baby. The mother had gone back into the mountains where she lived. Meanwhile, Elena had to stay at the orphanage in Guatemala until her mother could be found.

It took over a year to find her, but Elena's birth mother finally returned to the orphanage—this time with Rosa, Elena's baby sister. Liza and Derek were asked to adopt both girls instead of just one. "I was overwhelmed," Liza remembers, "full of both joy and terror at the same time. But . . . how could we say no to Elena's sister? [Soon] we were on a plane to Guatemala—and we came home with two daughters."

—Adapted from *Adoptive Parents* by Rae Simons (Mason Crest, 2010)

You may have a lot of questions about your birth parents. You might want to know why the adoption happened, or if you have siblings you've never met. If your adoption was open, you might be able to ask those questions directly. If not, it's okay to bring up these questions with your adoptive parents. They might not know all the answers, but they can probably help you begin to understand what happened. And if your birth family is from a different culture than your permanent family, you might be interested in learning more about that other culture.

Sometimes adopted kids are afraid to ask these questions. They don't want their adopted family to feel rejected. But it's natural to wonder about your birth family. Being curious about your past does not mean you are rejecting your present. It does not mean that you love your permanent family any less. It only means that you want to get a fuller understanding of who you are and where you came from.

If you are uncomfortable talking about these issues with your parents, consider finding another adult who can help, such as a teacher, a case worker from your adoption, or a leader from your church (if you have one). But in the end, it's important to remember that "real" family is not a matter of biology. Your real family are the people who love and support you day in and day out, regardless of what genetic material you share.

Text-Dependent Questions

1. What are some of the "core issues" of adoption?
2. Why is grief part of the adoption process?
3. What is a "sense of agency," and why does it matter?

Research Project

Research the phrase "alternative family tree project," and gather several designs that are commonly used, such as the wheel, the fan, and the rooted family tree. Try making one of each for your family. Which one did you like best? Which is the most inclusive?

FURTHER READING

Books

Gaskins, Pearl Fuyo. *What Are You?: Voices of Mixed-Race Young People.* New York: Henry Holt, 1999.

Harrison, Kathryn A. *Another Place at the Table.* New York: Jeremy P. Tarcher, 2003.

Merino, Noël, ed. *Adoption.* Introducing Issues with Opposing Viewpoints. Farmington Hills, MI: Greenhaven Press, 2008.

Simons, Rae. *Adoptive Parents.* Broomall, PA: Mason Crest, 2010.

Online

Belton, Danielle C. "3 Black Adoptees on Racial Identity after Growing Up with White Parents." *The Root,* January 27, 2015. http://www.theroot.com/articles/culture/2015/01/_3_black_adoptees_speak_about_growing_up_with_white_parents.html.

National Adoption Center. http://www.adopt.org/.

Silverstein, Deborah N. and Sharon Kaplan. "Lifelong Issues in Adoption." http://www.fairfamilies.org/2012/1999/99LifelongIssues.htm.

Get Help Now

Childhelp National Child Abuse Hotline

This free hotline is available 24-hours-a-day in 170 different languages.

1-800-4-A-CHILD (1-800-422-4453)   http://www.childhelp.org

SERIES GLOSSARY

agencies: departments of a government with responsibilities for specific programs.

anxiety: a feeling of worry or nervousness.

biological parents: the woman and man who create a child; they may or not raise it.

caregiving: helping someone with their daily activities.

cognitive: having to do with thinking or understanding.

consensus: agreement among a particular group of people.

custody: legal guardianship of a child.

demographers: people who study information about people and communities.

depression: severe sadness or unhappiness that does not go away easily.

discrimination: singling out a group for unfair treatment.

disparity: a noticeable difference between two things.

diverse: having variety; for example, "ethnically diverse" means a group of people of many different ethnicities.

ethnicity: a group that has a shared cultural heritage.

extended family: the kind of family that includes members beyond just parents and children, such as aunts, uncles, cousins, and so on.

foster care: raising a child (usually temporarily) that is not adopted or biologically yours.

heir: someone who receives another person's wealth and social position after the other person dies.

homogenous: a group of things that are the same.

ideology: a set of ideas and ways of seeing the world.

incarceration: being confined in prison or jail.

inclusive: accepting of everyone.

informally: not official or legal.

institution: an established organization, custom, or tradition.

kinship: family relations.

neglect: not caring for something correctly.

patriarchal: a system that is run by men and fathers.

prejudice: beliefs about a person or group based only on simplified and often mistaken ideas.

prevalence: how common a particular trait is in a group of people.

psychological: having to do with the mind.

quantify: to count or measure objectively.

restrictions: limits on what someone can do.

reunification: putting something back together.

secular: nonreligious.

security: being free from danger.

social worker: a person whose job is to help families or children deal with particular problems.

socioeconomic: relating to both social factors (such as race and ethnicity) as well as financial factors (such as class).

sociologists: people who study human society and how it operates.

spectrum: range.

stability: the sense that things will stay the same.

stereotype: a simplified idea about a type of person that is not connected to actual individuals.

stigma: a judgment that something is bad or shameful.

stressor: a situation or event that causes upset (stress).

traumatic: something that's very disturbing and causes long-term damage to a person.

variable: something that can change.

INDEX

Page numbers in *italics* refer to photographs or tables.

ABOUT THE AUTHOR

H. W. Poole is a writer and editor of books for young people, including the 13-volume set, *Mental Illnesses and Disorders: Awareness and Understanding* (Mason Crest). She created the *Horrors of History* series (Charlesbridge) and the *Ecosystems* series (Facts On File). She has also been responsible for many critically acclaimed reference books, including *Political Handbook of the World* (CQ Press) and the *Encyclopedia of Terrorism* (SAGE). She was coauthor and editor of *The History of the Internet* (ABC-CLIO), which won the 2000 American Library Association RUSA award.

PHOTO CREDITS

Photos are for illustrative purposes only; individuals depicted are models.
Cover: Dollar Photo Club/Somwaya
iStock.com: 6 Mordorlff; 9 Den Kuvaiev; 10 EdStock; 13 EdStock; 14 AleksandarNakic; 17 PeopleImages; 18 Portra; 28 Christopher Futcher; 30 Christopher Futcher; 33 Plougmann; 36 Susan Chiang; 38 Juanmonino; 41 Steve Debenport
Library of Congress: 23; 25
Wikimedia Commons: 20